A Work In Progress

A. Chuckalovchak

For family, for friends and for you.

Your love was not too hot
Not too cold
And that was the problem

My love for you was so hot
That it burnt me
Over and over

I deserve more
Than your room-temperature love

Afraid

Am I afraid of fear, or am I afraid of lack of fear?
Am I afraid of self-harm, or am I afraid of the thought of pain?
Am I afraid to give my all, or am I afraid of being let down?
Am I afraid of falling, or am I too afraid to look first?
Am I afraid of death, or am I afraid of "forever" ?
Am I afraid of pain, or am I afraid to be brave?
Am I afraid to accept, or am I afraid to deny facts?
Am I afraid of being alone, or am I afraid of silence?
Am I afraid of silence, or am I afraid of lack of sound?
Am I afraid to lose, or am I afraid to be a loser?
Am I afraid of being sad, or am I afraid of being seen like that?
Am I afraid of the absence of love, or am I afraid of the presence of hate?
Am I afraid at all, or am I afraid of the outcome of being fearless?

Like most females my age,
I am not a delicate flower.
I'm rather a tree.
I do not have pretty petals,
Nor do people constantly admire me.
I take pride in being a tree
Instead of a flower.
I have branches of all sorts,
I have names carved into me,
I have deep, strong roots.
Unlike delicate flowers,
I do not die or wilt easily,
I survive through storms,
I provide for others.
I'd much preferably be a tree
Than a flower.
I may not be beautiful,
Whimsical,
Or dainty.
But I am strong,
Rooted,
And resistant.

3 AM

You told me you loved me last night
But I knew you were drunk
It was 3 AM, and the words
Had rolled off your tongue
Like you were so certain
Like it was so easy
But I knew better
Young love is never certain
And no love is ever easy
I didn't know what to say
Because I knew it was only temporary
So I said that I was glad you loved me
And left it at that
And then you fell asleep

When you were drunk
You were in love with me
Then you woke up sober
And felt nothing but a hangover

Society

Don't be too skinny, and don't be too fat
Don't be an angel, and don't be a brat
Don't smile at everyone, and don't you dare frown
Don't act so happy, and don't act so down
Don't ever do drugs, and don't be a prude
Don't talk to strangers, and don't ever be rude
Don't act like you're perfect, and don't make mistakes
Don't be heartbroken, and don't cause heartbreaks
Don't cry all the time, and don't be emotionless
Don't have high expectations, and don't show hopelessness
Don't grow up, and don't forget that you're grown
Don't fall in love, and don't die alone
Don't forget your prescriptions, and don't pop any pills
Don't worry about finances, and don't forget to pay the bills
Don't worry too much, and don't be too laid back
Don't be racist, and don't mix white with black
Don't keep to yourself, and don't tell any secrets
Don't live on the edge, and don't have any regrets
Don't stop being humble, and don't be too proud
Don't be quiet, and don't be too loud
Don't forget to read the Bible, and don't try to push religion
Don't live life so strictly, and don't lack precision
Don't be arrogant, and don't hate yourself
Don't worry about money, and don't be clueless about wealth
Don't forget to pray before you sleep, and don't sleep 'till you're dead
Don't you know the monsters are surrounding you,
They're not under your bed

Die A Dreamer

And when my life starts approaching its end
I hope that
My laugh lines are deep crevices from smiling
My feet are worn soldiers from adventuring
My ring finger is imprinted from love
My brain is a novel full of knowledge
My thoughts are scattered from memories
My ankles are sore and fragile from dancing
My voice is a raspy jazz artist from singing
My heart aches from being so full
My stomach is a metal cage from holding butterflies
My eyes are Polaroid cameras from seeing beauty
I hope that
I don't die a dreamer
For that I have already made all of my dreams come true

Day One Without You.

    I have realized that I am completely consumed by you and by my thoughts of you. I cannot sleep. I cannot eat. I cannot breathe. I know you have caused me pain, but I pray to God you come back to me, even if it means to feel the pain over and over again. I fear that you won't ever come back, and I fear what will happen to me if you don't. I cannot live without you. You took the air out of my lungs and the heart out of my chest. This has been the longest day of my life and I can't help but wonder if these hours are dragging on for you, too.
I love you.

The odd thing about feelings is that sometimes,
I feel like I'm drowning in them.

In the middle of the ocean we call life.
I'm swimming in this ocean full of schoolwork, ex-lovers and painful words.
I'm swimming in this ocean full of memories, regrets, anxiety and nostalgia.
But I am not getting pulled back by any of it.
I swim so far away from it all that I don't have time to push it all under
the water.
I swim so rapidly that I don't even have a chance to think about them.
Once I get far enough, I look back at all of them at the same time.
They all bombard me at once from a distance.
So far from me that it all blends together.
I cannot tell which burden is the heaviest, so I see them all.
Getting battered by the waves crashing into me so relentlessly.
I cannot breathe.
And I drown.
I feel like I'm at the peak of anxiety.
I feel like my heart is dangerously close to shattering.
I feel like my mind is a ticking time bomb.

But, the weirdest thing about feelings is that sometimes,
I feel like I don't have any at all.

Yes, don't I look "okay"?
My hair is pulled up in an ideal bun,
not a single hair is out of place.
My lipstick isn't blotched or smudged.
My cheekbones look as defined as ever.
My mascara is beyond comparison,
eyelashes as long and shiny as a Cheshire cat's whiskers.
My outfit matches flawlessly and is very flattering on me.
My body stays strong, yet graceful.
Don't I look like I'm supposed to be on a magazine?
My doctor told me not to let your words hurt me.
My mother told me I should give you something to talk about.
My father told me to give you Hell.
Of course I'm okay.
I'm always okay.

Though

My hair is in a bun
because I couldn' t pull myself out of bed early enough to wash it.
My lipstick was applied at the very last minute in hopes that it would look
perfect.
My cheekbones look defined because I haven' t been able to eat in days without
getting sick.
My eyelashes look long because they are soaked with tears.
My outfit matches perfectly because I thought that
the stripe on polka-dot pattern would display my emotions too obviously.
My strong body holding up with great posture and poise is trembling and
shaking.
My doctor told me that I would be okay.
My mother told me that I would be okay.
My father told me that I would be okay.
The voices in my head even tell me that I would be okay.
Are YOU okay?

I may be unstable.
I may be a mess.
I may even be a train wreck.
But you will never know.
Instead, I will tell you what you hate to hear.
Of course I' m okay.
I' m
Always
Okay.

Breathing in through her nose, out through her mouth.
Hearing the music in the background as the lyrics went into
Her ears and twirled around her mind like a ballerina.
The top was down on the car, the wind blowing through her
Knotted hair.
A flask was in her left hand, a dandelion behind her ear.
She sat in the backseat with her eyes slightly closed,
Mouth pursed with sweetness.
She believed in peace and rainbows.
She believed n happiness and sunshine.
She was exactly who she dreamed of being.
She was exactly where she wanted to be.
The crazy, wild, flower child.

-Bliss

You and I are not the same.

I'm more like a red dress on a Saturday night.
Like a worthless cigarette butt on a busy sidewalk.
Like a favorite pair of heels that were broken from being danced in.
Like bright red lipstick on a shining face.
Like a kite on the beach during a day that the wind refuses to blow.
Like a rain drop in a drought.
Like an empty box that was given as a gift.
Like the very first firefly of the summer to get put in the mason jar.
Like a song that gets overplayed.
But I'm more like a red dress on a Saturday night.

What color dress are you?

Lonely

I'm losing more than I intended to, and gaining hardly anything at all.
And to think, I lost some of the people that would catch me when I fall.
I lost some that I loved, and they lost me back, and to think, all we have are memories.
A picture, a sigh, a wave goodbye, they were such dear friends to me.
I'm losing grip without effort, as I am watching them slip on by.
Sometimes I have the urge to be mad, sometimes the urge to cry.
So this is for all the people, who used to matter most.
I learn from my mistakes, and from now on, I am keeping my "close friends" close.

Darling, let me make it clear. Not even a diamond could keep me here.

Here's to the people who sit in their room with all of the lights off, staring at their ceiling thinking of everything and nothing all at the same time.

Here's to the people that want to escape everything and never go back.

Here's to the people who get judged for being too perfect, yet get shunned because you aren't good enough for others.

Here's to the people who suffer from eating disorders and just cannot bring themselves to take a bite of that one thing that they have been craving.

Here's to the people that do self-harm, not for attention, but because they need to remember what it's like to feel at all.

Here's to the people who love the same gender, but stay alone for the rest of their lives because society doesn't allow them to love who they want to love freely.

Here's to the people who sit alone in class, but always have eyes on them and are constantly laughed at or talked about.

Here's to the people who get harassed at school every day and want to drop out because you would rather live an uneducated life than a constantly sad one.

Here's to the people who have been physically and emotionally abused by a loved one and could not escape it.

Here's to the people that don't feel comfortable in their own skin.

Here's to the people that put down the drugs, gun, knife, rope and told themselves that they are beyond that.

This is not for the prom queens, the partiers, the abusers, the jocks, the bullies, or the people that never gave you the chance to be good enough.

This is for the people who have overcame diversity.

This is for the people who never get credit from anyone who live their day-to-day lives with pain or worry.

This is for the people who deserve all the credit in the world and get none at all.

This is for you.

I am proud of you.

I walked into the crowded room
As everybody stared.
I tried not to read the deceiving faces,
The smiles and the glares.
I was wearing my shortest dress I owned,
Hoping to be noticed.
I actually applied makeup tonight,
To act like I'm not at my lowest.
The talking pulsed through my bones,
The music was in my veins.
I shut my eyes and felt the vibes.
I forgot all of my pain.
I wasn't supposed to go out tonight,
Especially not alone.
But I needed to get out of my own head
And my friends wouldn't pick up their phones.
They knew I was at my breaking point.
They knew I needed them.
They left me alone, I couldn't stay home.
All I wanted was a friend.
I danced all night on the dance floor,
Alone with all my thoughts.
This type of thing wasn't my scene,
But I kept on taking shots.
As a cute guy across the room
Saw me catch his glare,
I blushed a bit and smiled,
As I sexily tousled my hair.
He grabbed my hips and kissed my lips
As we became one on the dance floor.
I kept accepting the drinks he gave me.
His charming smile made me want more.
One thing lead to another,
But after another, I forget.
Looking down and seeing the boy now,
I know he has no regrets.
My friends can no longer call me.
I can no longer go out.
I broke every rule that they taught me,

If my parents could talk to me they'd shout.
The police found me in an ally.
The cute boy nowhere to be found.
My friends regret not coming with me.
They knew I needed them around.
Everyone is blaming me,
I went to a party alone.
I drank whatever was handed to me,
I let a stranger take me home.
I'm assuming when the tests come back,
The boy will say I asked for it.
I should have never worn that short dress,
Or danced as risqué as I did.
Maybe it was the hair flip,
Or the wink that I went wrong.
Maybe it's because I nodded my head
When he said we would leave after the song.
They tasted just like normal drinks,
I couldn't tell they were drugged.
The boy just seemed so innocent
Through his smiles and his hugs.
My body was too small to handle
All the doses I consumed.
It didn't seem like a huge surprise
When dead, I was presumed.
The boy will move on with his life,
For he didn't even know my name.
I'm the only girl he got to
That wasn't able to do the walk of shame.
Partying was dangerous like they said
While teaching rape and drug prevention.
But I don't know how us victims get blamed,
I guess I should have paid more attention.

There is something so captivating about a person that is sleeping.
They become so innocent and carefree.
They escape. And you can watch them do it.
You can witness them enter another realm outside of reality.
Infants sleep and killers sleep.
I believe that there is nothing more paradoxically beautiful than that.

Positivity is a crutch that can hold even the weakest person up.
Persistence is a path that can end the darkest beginning with the brightest end.
Happiness is a rehab that can take away the worst addicts pain.
Love is a clock that makes your time go forward.
You are a warrior that can take any path, any way, at any time.
So what's stopping you?

A Girl's Best Friend

Diamonds shine and sparkle
Like your teeth just never would.
Diamonds can be replaced
But I know you never could.
Diamonds get shown off so well
Your bark drew all the attention
Diamonds wouldn't dig in the trash
Or do other things I won't mention.
Diamonds won't wake me up by kissing my face or nibbling my toes
Diamonds won't cuddle me at night
Or play tug and crinkle it's nose.
Diamonds won't drag me by a leash
When we go out on a jog.
Whoever said diamonds were a girl's best friend
Clearly never had a dog.

If some day, you forget me, I'll be fine with that. But I hope you stumble across foggy memories from time to time that make you sense an overwhelming wave of happiness.

A lesson.

Learn how to fall out of love faster than you can fall in love, or learn how to not love at all.

My stomach aches from the butterflies
My head is clouded with dreams
My happiness is concealed with your lies
Nothing is at all as it seems

I know that if you had known
That our last kiss
Was going to be our last
For good this time
You would have held onto me a little tighter
And made it last a little longer
If I knew
That I had finally become strong enough
To make it our last kiss
That I would have whispered
 "good riddance" while our foreheads
were still welded together
as if they would never part
and I would have made damn sure
that when I pulled away from you
for that very last time
that you would have fucking felt it

I looked at myself in the mirror
Tears were already running down my face,
My drab dress draped on my cold skin.

I don't look good in black.

He didn't even like the color black.

He didn't like anything about the color black.

He liked yellow and orange
He liked sports and music
He liked people and parties
He liked everything

But I don't think he liked the color black.

He would have told me that I looked good in it anyways.

But I don't.

I know I don't.

I will walk into a room full of crying people.
The whole crowd crying except him
But this will be the first time he isn't smiling
The first time he isn't looking at me
With his big, bright, brilliant eyes

I will pick up the paper sitting by the doorway
With his name, young age and picture on the front
I will accidentally crumple the paper up
Clenching it in my sweaty, shaking hands

I will look at him.

When he's laying still,

He will look the same
His eyebrows will be big and bushy
His brown hair will be cut to perfection
His lips will be pursed with sweetness

But when he's laying still

How will I look up at him
As he would open his long, slender arms
And bend over so he could be the same height as me
So he could hold me in his warm embrace

When he's laying still,
How will he be telling me stories
Whispering sweet nothings in my ear
Telling me silly jokes through his laughter
Singing songs with me

Everyone in the room will say a prayer together
His basketball coach will tell stories of him
His parents and family will weep
The whole town will unite
And we all will cry

I will tell him goodbye
Even though I know he won't say it back
I will shut my eyes for a brief moment
And imagine what he was like the week before
More full of life than anyone I had ever known

Half of him will be lying in front of me
While the other half of him will be looking down on me
And the angel he is will smile and say

"You look good in black".

In memory of Dominick L. Wilgus. I love you always.

Arhus

My bike peddles are going faster
Than my brain will let me process
The people
The places
The things I am seeing
That I never thought I would see
The things I am feeling
That I never thought I would feel
The lessons I am teaching myself
The lessons I am learning from complete strangers
The lessons I will carry for the rest of my life
Are not even in the country that I reside in

I have smiled until it hurt
Though I have never known my worth
I have laughed until I cried
Though my pain was masked with pride
I have pushed until I was done
Though I hated who I had become
I have loved until I lost
Though I never knew the cost
How beautiful would it be
To be able to let everyone see
How we feel rather than look
Because I know I don't look shook
But, my dear, I have been rattled
Until my entire being shattered
And I can't allow anyone to see
Because no one can know the real me

The moment that I looked into my mother's eyes
Through my eyes filled with tears
And said to her with a tremor in my voice
 "This is the reason people kill themselves"
Was the moment I realized
That I am stronger than any other person
I have ever met.
In that moment I realized
I have never picked up a razor
Other than to shave my legs
I have never handled a knife
Other than to cut the food I am lucky to have
I have played tug of war
With my heart and head
But never with a rope and my neck
I have never pulled the trigger on a gun
Other than to fire paintballs
I have never taken too many pills
Or held my breath too long
Or turned my car on inside my garage
Or jumped off of things that were incredibly high
Or drove my car too fast
In that moment I realized
That I am stronger than any other person
In that moment I realized
That I am a warrior

You can run until your legs are sore,
Your lungs are tired,
And your head is empty.
You can fight until your fists are bruised,
Your knees are weak,
And you feel defeated
You can deny until you're blue in the face
But your problems will fight you.
Life will chase you.
And you will find yourself.

I got the phone call that someone was worried about him.
Asking me if I saw the white in his nose.
Asking me if I saw the marks on his arm.
Asking me if I was worried too.
He told me not to tell his parents.
I said I wouldn't.
He thanked me.
I got the phone call that he needed money today.
Right now.
Immediately.
I rushed to his house and called him when I pulled into the gravel driveway.
I stared at the trailer for what felt like years.
He told me I couldn't come in.
I emptied my wallet for him.
He thanked me.
I got the phone call that he was in jail.
I rushed to the jailhouse and pulled him out.
He thanked me.
I got the phone call that he was passed out at a party.
I hesitantly walked into the basement.
I saw him face down on a table.
With lines of white surrounding him
And a tied rubber band around his forearm.
I carried him out and took him home.
He thanked me.
I got the phone call that he wasn't going to get help.
That I was all the help he needed.
I told him that he needed something more.
He refused.
He thanked me.
I got the phone call that he was incoherent in an ally downtown.
I drove 90 miles per hour to get to him.
I walked alone down every dark ally until I found him.
Slumped over by a dumpster.
Wallet empty.
Skin splotchy and cold.
Teeth brittle.
Chest still.
He didn't thank me.
And I no longer got any phone calls.

Time

I was never afraid of time
Until my best friend died and time stood still.
And my grandpa was told he had cancer and I wanted to rewind.
And the love of my life left for basic training and I wanted to fast forward.
And I had my first kiss and wanted to pause.
And I got my heart broken and realized time went too fast.
I was never afraid of time
Until I realized that it has nothing to do with numbers on a clock
And it has everything to do with how you live your life when the clock is
ticking.

Maybe I like my coffee black
Because that's the shade of my soul
Or I am going through a hard time
Or I see darkness all around me
Maybe I like my coffee black
Because my childhood was moonless
Or I don't like anything sweet
Or I'm inconsolable

Maybe I like my coffee black
Because I like my fucking coffee black

−I see you staring at me across the coffee shop
with judgment based off of the only thing you know about me

I have never said that I was glad that I didn't exit my comfort zone. No growth comes if you stay in it.
Jump on the airplane.
Kiss the boy.
Call the ex.
Take the shot.
Get on stage.
Wear the skirt.
Dance with the stranger.
Miss the train.
Be alone.
Wake up.
Leave the comfort zone.
Don't go back.
Run.
& run.
& run.

The funeral

My insecurities are the casket that I'm burying myself in.
I want them to be the dead in me, but they always seem to win.

I put up this fight all of my life and it took me to my grave.
Diffidence was stronger than confidence & my self-doubt was not saved.

My ex-lovers at my entombment, saying they wish I believed their truths.
My family members unalarmed because I've been in the casket since youth.

My friends with blood dripping off their fingers with sweaty, shaky hands.
They tried & tried to destroy my casket, though that wasn't friendship's plan.

The love of my life gazing at it, asking, "what more could I have done?
I told her she was beautiful, she was my diamond, my heart, my sun."

My insecurities are the casket of what I could be and what I have been.
Dragging others in with me because my timidity lured them in.

I tried to kill my insecurities before they could kill me.
Though I kicked & screamed & tore at the seams, my casket stayed sturdy.

What wasn't in the casket was my will to fight this fate.
The casket will eventually break, it is never too late.

My insecurities are the casket that I'm burying myself in.
I will make them be the dead in me, I refuse to let them win.

I know that the sun has been setting earlier lately
And everything has been a repetitive motion.
Your coffee is always too hot to drink
And the books you have been reading are predictable.
Everything seems hazy
And your world is spinning
But standing still at the same time.

But darling I promise;

The sun will still rise in the morning
Perhaps even higher than it did yesterday.
The coffee will cool
And the next novel will surprise you.
The haze will fade away
And the world will stay in motion
Just like it always has
Just like it always will.

isn' t it odd
that your darkest shadows
only appear
when you are
facing towards
the sunlight

It ate me alive,
From the inside
Out
Rummaging through
Each
Emotion
Sucking the energy from my
Chest
Reaping the pain in
Each
Heart
Beat
Beat
Beat
And now it seems
Beat
Like I cannot do anything
Beat
Without this
Beat
Beat
Beat
Coming out of my chest

Stop telling me to vote
Stop telling me to hate gays
Stop telling me to not be attracted to black men
Stop telling me to go vegan
Stop telling me we are equal
Stop telling me to keep my mouth shut
When none of you can keep your mouths shut
Stop telling me to censor myself
When you are anything but censored
When America is anything but censored
The government is making me walk a pin-straight line
When the government is the most crooked line I have ever seen

Prague

I can hear the ghostly footsteps
Of my great grandmother running to pack her bags
When Nazi Germany pushed in
I can feel my great grandfather's childhood
Get picked up and thrown to America
I can feel the aura
Of my ancestors before me
Crying with joy
For the life that they built me
Maybe it was the familiar taste of
Budweiser on my lips
Maybe it was the way the faint music
Sounded like my grandmother's hums
Maybe it was the cobblestone on my feet
That made me feel so grounded

Life is so fragile
Delicate
Intricate
And just like that,
You get an expiration date
Like life is nothing more than a jug of milk

2017

I am white and I am mad at white people
I am pro choice and I am mad at everyone's choices
I am educated and I am mad at our education system
I am a female and I am mad at feminists
I am a believer and I am mad at Christians
I am an American and I am mad at America

3:47 AM

my anxiety is pouring out of my body and drowning the entire world

You can only turn over a new leaf so many times
before autumn comes to an end

A Letter To My Father's Father

I spent my entire life trying to be gold for you
When all you could do was tell me how beautiful silver is

A Letter To My Mother's Father

I spent my entire life trying to be gold for you
When you thought that I was gold without effort

You may need your biology to survive
But cancer of the soul is impossible
And you need nothing but your spirit to live

An Open Letter To My Anxiety

You made me late for work today. You made me make sure all the knobs on the oven were set to "off" seven times even though I haven't cooked in three days. You made me "locked, locked, locked, locked, locked, locked, locked" all three doors in my house. You made me drive five miles under the speed limit because there were exactly twenty-one things that could have gone wrong if I didn't. you made me shake and I can't tell if it's directly caused by you or because I overused my albuterol because 23 years later I still don't know the difference between my asthma and you. You made my mom cry. You made my grandma worry. You made my boyfriend feel helpless when I told him there was nothing he could do even though he tries so hard to kick you out. I have spent so much time ignoring your presence that even when you're running your fingers through my hair and knitting a scarf for my heart with barbed wire I still can't even tell if you are here or not. You have made me feel guilty. Guilty for gaining weight. Guilty for occasionally needing medicine just for you to use your manners for one night. Guilty of sleeping for twelve hours straight and waking up too exhausted to get up. Guilty for feeling the way I do today because I swear to God, the God you refuse to believe in or trust, that I am the happiest person alive. You have haunted my nights and halted my days and I can't see you or touch you but I know you weigh a thousand pounds when you are sitting on my chest and I know that you only intended on vacationing here but you got so comfortable that you resided in me instead but I need you to know that you are not welcome here. And since you cannot leave, be quiet. Because I'm in charge now.

You could stab my back a hundred more times
and I would still ask if you needed help
washing my blood off of the knife

I had a nightmare last night
About a beautiful, yet evil monster
It took away my whole soul
And shattered my entire heart
The monster was not even that scary
It really had a way with words
It actually made me feel safe for a while
What a surprise that something so
Destructive could be so warm
But I'll call it a nightmare
Rather than a dream
Because
Your voice still haunts me

It isn't easy

To appreciate

The sunrise

That wakes you

When you're

Running

On three

Hours of sleep

And a

Broken

Heart

Goodnight.

My hand meets his
I feel a rush
It feels like Heaven when we touch
He pushes my hair back
Looks in my eye
His stare alone can make me high
He grins at me
I can't help but stare
I lose my breath and can't get air
His lips touch mine
I lose my mind
I know its love, though love is blind
He wraps his arms around me
Like I'm in a cocoon
My heart gets warmer than the month of June
He tells me he loves me
I then say it back
I see stars though the room is indeed pitch black
He closes his eyes
Then I close mine
With chills still running down my spine
He dozes off quickly
I take my time with the deal
For I don't have to sleep so my dreams can be real
I look over at him
I smile and laugh
Because I know that I found my other half

But your love was never as strong
As my arms
When I was trying to
Hold onto you
And your love was never as deep
As the pit
That formed in my stomach
When you left me

He will put the keys in the ignition
And start this crazy ride
That some may call a "relationship"
He will put his foot on the gas lightly
Until I am comfortable enough
For him to slam the pedal to the ground
More rapidly than I believed was possible
Then he will slam on the brakes
When we are on the smoothest part of the road
For no reason
With no remorse
He will buckle my seatbelt for me
So I will feel safer with him
Than I ever have in my entire life
He will give me the wheel
And let me drive him crazy
Until he loses all control
To the point of insanity
And we keep missing all the exits
And I sit there
Stuck in that damn seatbelt that
He fastened so tightly
And he will hop out of the car
And leave me inside
Alone
Suffocating
Stuck
And he will walk away
And he will not look back at
The wreck he has left me in

Your scent dances around my blankets and pillows
The same way we danced through them together at night
Your pictures hang perfectly on the walls and stare at me
The same way you stare at me when I speak
Your face is embedded in my mind
The same way I can hear your "I love you"s on command
You hold my entire heart
The same way you cradle me every time we sleep
Your voice lingers in my mind
The same way your words hang onto your lips
Your clothes are a mess on my floor
The same way we thought our relationship would be
Your eyes illuminate my entire world
The same way you say that mine do yours
You are absolutely perfect
The same way our relationship ended up being
I love you
The same way you love me

The mistake you made was
You cared about yourself more than you cared about
Other people
You cared about things
That would make you feel temporary happiness
You spent time caring
About things that cannot care back
Things that all will disappear
Things that will never last or matter
Things that will slowly dwindle with time
And never come back
But then you only have yourself
You only love yourself
You only care about yourself
And when you die
It's all over
And you will never realize
The selfish mistake that you had made
You will never realize
That you lost yourself
Long before you were even gone
And you were too busy
Loving things that cannot love you back
Almost as much as you loved yourself
To realize that you had lost yourself
Somewhere
Down the road
And maybe even realize
That you never really had yourself
In the first place

She never believed the lies that poured out of your lips like poison
She never fell for the words that rolled off your tongue like the sweetest drug
She never doubted that she could lose you at any moment
She never was sure that everything was okay
She never thought the future you spoke of was possible
But she hoped.
And she hoped.
And she hoped.

Amalfi

The water was freezing
And I jumped in
The alcohol was strong
And I gulped it
The stray animals were unpleasant
And I held them
The roads were narrow
And I walked them
This is the most beautiful place I have ever seen

We were as hot as mid-summer in Texas
My emotions blew around like a stormy day in Chicago
We shone as bright as a spring day in Florida
I was trapped like a snowstorm in New York
You changed like the seasons in Ohio
I was shaken up like an earthquake in California
My tears flooded like a rainstorm in Washington
You turned me as cold as a winter night in Wyoming
Those winters were brutal
The summers were unbearable
The falls were intense
See, I went all around the country for you
When you wouldn't even take a damn step for me

Your fence-like love gave me limits,
But I could never break them down.
Your stormy ways set me back sometimes,
But I never turned around.
Your thunder words had hurt me,
But I acted like I didn't hear a sound.
Your lightening looks pierced my soul,
But I tried to just look down.
You were the storm of the century,
The chaos of my world.
The wildest tornado in my heart,
And around our relationship whirled.
Your storm changed like the seasons,
So often I never knew
If you were the eye of the storm or the calm
But away my feelings blew.
I see people hide from the rain.
I see people run from the thunder.
I see lightening cause people pain.
I see people stare at tornados with wonder.
I grew far too accustomed to your storms.
I was actually far too brave.
So I decided to wait the storm out
But not let it take me to my grave.
My happiness came when you went away.
I'll still think of you every rainy day.

The scary thing about love is that you don't need two people in order to feel it.
You can love all you want but the other person may not love you back.
The scary thing about love is that it can disappear.
One day you can write a novel about the definition of love, the next you can be empty.
The scary thing about love is that it is not permanent like people say it is.
Not only can you fall out of love, you can completely forget what it felt like.
You can actually look into the eyes of someone you once loved, and feel nothing.
You can forget love. You can lose love. You can love alone.
But the only love that is eternal is the love that you have for yourself.
That can never go away.

I remember time before you.

I did whatever I wanted, happily.

Then I met you.

I smiled and laughed, I bettered myself, I danced around my room.

And you're gone.

Now all I seem to do,

Is drink coffee, write sad poems, whisper bad words, and wait.

Oh, how I wish you could know
Everything that I will never tell you.
How your smile made me melt like the snow.
How your eyes were my favorite view.
Oh, how I wish you could see
Everything that I will never show you.
The scars that line my wrists perfectly
Or the marks on my neck that are black and blue.
Oh, how I wish you could hear
The words I will never speak to you.
 "I'm only myself when you're near" or
 "I really am in love with you."
Oh, how I wish you could taste
The things you never will taste again.
My lips will never be replaced.
Neither will the bitterness of that cheap champagne.
Oh, how I wish you could feel
The spark we used to ignite.
When we held hands, it felt so real.
Or when we made love after the fights.
Oh, how I wish you could remember
The things I am trying to forget
How we fell in love in December
And shared rich dreams despite our debt.
Oh, how I wish I could speak to you
Though it will not happen again.
When your love for us lessened, mine grew.
Maybe in another life, my friend.

Sometime, you will realize that enough
Is
Enough.
The pain and hurting
Is
Enough.
Staying up all night
Is
Enough.
The tears that run down your cheek
Is
Enough.
Whatever he gave you
Wasn't
Enough.
Sometime, you will realize that
You
Are
More
Than
 "Enough."

Withdrawal

If love was a drug, I hadn't been sober in months.
Now I know a thing or two about withdrawal.
If only he knew how intoxicated I was.

Munich

The train is packed
I almost missed it
I am drenched with rain and sweat
I cannot understand a word
I do not know where I am headed
I am drunk off of beer and confusion
I am homesick but don' t want to leave
I have no idea what is going on
But I do know that I am free

As we sat on your couch, avoiding
Eye contact for the first time since
Our first date when we were both
More nervous than we had ever been
I twiddled my thumbs and I
Held back tears until my pupils burnt
Like the time I got sand in my eyes
When we were at the beach
And my hands shook just like
They did whenever you kissed me
And I could barely contain myself
And my breath quivered as it did
Whenever we exchanged "I love you"
The first time
And I did not have any idea who was
Sitting on that couch with me
Like the night we met at that party
And we knew nothing about each other
Except that we had chemistry yet
This time, you know me and
I know you and I also know
We have no chemistry
And I know how your veins pop out when
You are mad at me and I know
How you talk to other girls when I'm
Not around you and I know
How you clench your jaw
When I talk too much and I know
How you look to the left when you lie
And I know that all you have done
The past few months is look to the left
And look to the left and look to the left
And we can sit here on your couch
For as long as you want to but we
Both know too much about each other
And we both know that it is over
And it has been over
Since the first time we sat on this couch
But we will sit here in silence and
Avoid eye contact and act like we aren't
Confused as hell that everything was
Perfect until we actually knew each other

Sweden

The trees are blowing the same as home
Though it is from a different wind
I am the same person when I am here
My shoulders still carry my sins
The people here do not know me
Which is exactly what I had hoped
I feel more at-peace here
Though I am still hopelessly toped
The moon I see is still the same
On the other side of the world
I do not have any history here
I am just "some girl"
The water is still as my silence
The air here suffocates me less
I wish I could say that I miss home
But right now, I feel too blessed

"What a terrible cycle to be in" I thought to myself
as I stared at my ceiling.
I have gone from
being afraid to talk to you,
to being afraid to care about you,
to being afraid to get serious with you,
to being afraid to lose you
to being afraid to talk to you
all over again.
The cycle will repeat, and repeat, and repeat.
Like a broken record.
And if this is what love is; this cycle with no pattern other than constantly
being afraid,
I would rather not love at all.

Someday, I want a man to look at me like I am the most beautiful mess in the world.

I want a man that can sit in silence with me for hours with our bare legs intertwined.

I want a man that knows how I like my coffee, and knows how I look at my left foot when I'm nervous.

I want a man that knows all my freckles, and traces my birthmark with his index finger as he admires my crooked smile.

I want a man that knows what all my scars are from, and embraces each individual piece of the raised, unappealing skin.

I want a man that cannot keep his hands off of me, and doesn't ever try to.

I want a man that will sit on the couch and have a beer with me when the game is on.

I want a man that works hard, and expects me to work hard, as well.

I want a man that loves himself, loves me, and loves us.

I want a man that is strong enough to not hold back my strengths.

I want a man that yells with me when I am too loud, whispers when I am too quiet, smiles when I am laughing and breaks when I am too broken.

I want a man that loves me unconditionally.

Week One Without You.

　　I have not seen your face or heard your voice in days, but I can still shut my eyes and picture you perfectly. My constant crying has turned into permanent numbness and anger. I am able to leave the house now and I can manage to tell people that I'm all right even though they know I'm lying. I'm trying to give myself hope that we aren't completely done because the thought of living the rest of my life without you is driving me mad. Maybe this is real and you won't come back. Maybe you will, though. Maybe I am still consumed by you, because I still cannot breathe.
I love you.

He appreciated me
He admired my art
And let every word I ever wrote
Resonate with his soul
He admired my body
Like it was art itself
He traced over every scar
With a compliment
He closed every wound
With support
He never told me he loved me
But I know that he loved me
More than anyone has
More than anyone will
More than I could love myself
I know that he loved me
So how could I have let him go

Excuses

growing up, I was told
 "don' t make excuses for yourself"
but growing up, I was never told
 "don' t make excuses for other people"
so I didn' t know better
all I knew was to not make excuses
for myself
maybe that' s why
I made so many excuses
for why you left

I woke up beside him and smiled
Because he is so mesmerizing
He brushed his hand across my cheek
Meek as if he was not powerful enough
To make me lose my breath
I got shivers down every inch of my spine
As I always do when he caresses me
I feel like our souls align
We are soulmates, perhaps
And I am happy
But not as happy as I have been before
He is wonderful
He treats me like a queen
He is a beautiful soul
And
He will never have a clue
How much I am still in love with you

& isn't it horrifyingly beautiful
That desolation & love correlates better
Than desolation & loneliness

Captivated by your touch
When will all of this be too much

Why can' t enough ever just be enough
I never want to let go

It' s hard for me to sympathize
When you look in my eyes and lie to me

I know you' re over hearing me cry
And honestly I' m exhausted

It' s hard to know when to cut the ties
When I' m in such a position

I' m telling you that I' ll be gone for good
Can you hear me? Do you ever listen?

Knowing I' ll be miserable without you
And miserable with you, hurts

Now I must decipher
Which "miserable" is worse

Sometimes the person that throws
In the towel

Is the person that wins the game
All I know is in this diversion

You are the one to blame

Oxygen

When he leaves, he does not take your oxygen.
Show him that.

Denmark

Planes, trains, metros and cars
I travel the world & still
Don't know where you are
I roll past the trees
The faces all blur
The schedules all mesh
Nothing is for sure
I'm living it up
I'm drinking it down
If this is a race
You can take the crown
I love the moving
I love painting the skies blue
I love passing boundaries
And I love you

I lost track of who you were
When you became my heart
I cannot tell when it happened
Maybe you have been different from the start
I lost track of who you were
When you became my soul
It didn' t matter what you were doing
I thought you made me whole
I lost track of who you were
When you became my air
You filled my lungs with what I needed
You were everywhere
I lost track of who you were
Because I loved you so much
I did not know your evil intentions
Hidden in every touch
I lost track of who you were
So much I had no clue
That the person I thought you really were
Was not really you

I want to tell you that I don't remember the sound of your voice. I don't want you to know that it still echoes through the silence.

I want to tell you that I wonder how you have been. I don't want you to know that I have been looking at your social media daily.

I want to tell you that I burned all your photos. I don't want you to know that I have them all in my desk drawer.

I want to tell you that I'm happy you moved on. I don't want you to know that I constantly wonder if she is prettier, funnier, nicer or smarter than me.

I want to tell you that I'm okay. I don't want you to know that I have cried every day since we exchanged somber goodbyes.

I want to tell you that I hate you. I don't want you to know how much I love you.

Curiosity may have killed the cat, but I doubt it did anything to the dog.

No one loves the life they live because it's perfect, they love the life they live because they choose to.

Addiction killed her.
He pulsed through her veins
He was in her blood
He festered in her once-beautiful soul
Until it turned to an empty black vessel
She slowly fell apart
More and more each day
The withdrawal after he left
Tore her apart even more
He still ran throughout her

You only come over to get
Your fix.
But then,
Your scent dances through my sheets
For weeks on end.
And I find myself
Holding the pillow
Your head rested on
When you whispered that
you missed me
and you traced my lips
with your finger.
And suddenly
Silence sounds so much better
Than music
Coffee has a bitter taste
The cold weather no longer
Bothers me
And I can never tell whether
My heart is
Jumping or sinking.

My heart cannot be put on the line
again for someone who has
nothing to offer it.

Year One Without You.

I have grown so much as a person without you. I never thought that would be possible. I saw you around a few times and we were back at square one, then we part to act like we don't know each other for a few more months. I'm fine with that.

Though I am fine without you, I find myself not being able to be with anyone else.

Maybe you are my soul mate.

Maybe you are the love of my life.

Maybe I am destined to be alone.

Though I cannot imagine us being together again, I cannot even fathom the thought of being with anyone but you. I smile and I laugh now. I carry on with my own life and am so happy with where I am. I am happy with where you are. I don't think of you often, not even every day anymore - which makes me sadder than anything else because I no longer remember what your laugh sounds like, or what your lips feel like, or how hearing you say my name feels. But I do think of you from time to time. I feel like I always will. But I am fine without you. Though I am fine now without you, when I think of you, I get that beastly feeling in my stomach and I still cannot breathe.

I will be fine if I never see you again in my life.

I love you.

Since the end of us,
I have had more bodies crawl through
these sheets than I'd like to admit
Yet my bed has felt empty since you left.

(October)

the leaves are starting to fall,
baring everything that has been hidden all season.
The weather is getting cold:
Slowly, but then all at once.
nature is falling apart, really.
But it is so serene and beautiful.
I think people have Octobers, too.

Running on Empty

I tapped my pen on my desk for hours
I stared at my vibrant wall
I was grey
I had no purpose
My paper was bare, begging to be inscribed on
But I was no more than a blank canvas begging to be etched on myself
I had everything
But felt nothing
My life was full
But I was empty
I was four walls full of blank space
As he walked out he told me
    "At least now you have something to write about"

where I came from

I was built with recycled tears
Empty hopes
And a long line of sinners
I was created with passion
Endless dreams
And a decision
I was molded with the hands of God himself
My mother's intuition
And my father's bad habits
I was formed with a thirst for knowledge
A curiosity that remains unmatched
And a heart that never stops racing

When people live in black and white
You beg them to show their colors.
When people show their colors
You admit that they are too bright.
But even the sunset is breathtaking
When it is behind a different lens.

The Illusion

His hand seemed to mold to my throat
Much easier than it did my hand
But he had always wrapped his arms around me
With love tight enough to leave bruises
I can tell that there is passion in every thrust
Because the pain overflows my entire body
And he always covers my mouth
And tells me to stop crying
But we are making love
His heavy hands work so hard for me
As well as on me
Enough to take my breath away
He is always taking my breath away
I call him handsome
He calls me wretched
I call him amazing
He calls me ignorant
I call him
He never answers
Thank god I have a man who loves me

at one point, i thought i would fail out of college

my grandpa would say
"you are as smart as you allow yourself to be"

and something clicked
my gears began turning
my stomach began churning
and my mind started rolling like roll-ball on a roulette table and i have no
idea where the final thought will end up but i know that ball can either make
me or break me once it stops rolling so please god never let it stop rolling

my brain is a library full of beautiful poetry
i can recite half of shakespears pieces and i can tell my future children
about symphonies and textbooks alike as well as exactly what Goodnight Moon
says to them as i tuck them into bed but i am far too young and far too
uneducated to have a child yet

i have to have a degree to be able to get pregnant not a husband it doesnt
matter that i can change diapers in 30 seconds flat or know exactly what to
expect when i'm expecting or know that a bottle needs to be 98 degrees because
if i cant pass intermediate math the first time around how could i possibly be
smart enough to start a family

i can tell you every drug and what they do to your body - no really - exactly
what happens to your body and i might not have the epi pen, the narcan, the
rehab that you need but i have ears and sometimes thats all people like you
need from people like me

my mind is as quick as a cheetah chasing after its prey but once i get to my
prey i suddenly dont feel hungry anymore however i have a thirst for knowledge
that never goes away like when i get an A on a project that i made myself sick
over every single night yet the second after my A gets submitted into the
portal that my professor cant figure out yet i feel like i still don't know
enough when my hand violently scratches words into my notebook the next day
during lecture

i can copy notes almost as fast as i can type and when i type my mind takes a photo and i can see it clear as day on any day except the day that i have tests over the material

i can write a book on everything i learned in gender studies, business 101, lifespan development and my last relationship but all that matters is that my 30 page paper on something i dont know about is cited properly and formatted just like they said and if my punctuation is off because the six cups of coffee called my nerves made me shake then i don't even deserve a grade showing that i spilled all my time and energy learning about something that i cant get a handle on

i missed every family dinner this week because i was too busy doing research and i missed my cousins volleyball game because i was too busy writing a reference page and i miss my mother and my dog and my sanity but you do not seem to care about anything other than my punctuation

i am an empty chalk board that professors have been writing on for four years and there is nothing drawn on me but percentages and discouragement

i am a bachelors degree that mutters "what about the masters" and the masters degree is standing in line behind me staring at the clock laughing when people say "it's never too late" and the PhD is standing behind masters begging me to come to the back of the line and stand with him but my dreams are at the front of the line and i want to stay at the front of the line so badly but i'm not sure if that even matters

my grandpa told me
"you are as smart as you allow yourself to be"

society told me
"try again"

and the moment i walked across that stage to get the paper that says my name on it and means nothing but a minimum wage job offer

i realized that my grandfather was not always right

My mind wanders as much as my feet
Waking up with wanderlust on repeat
I try so hard to never sleep
So my dreams can become my lifestyle

I walk barefoot and I talk loud
A bright red blip in a grey cold crowd
Only trying to make myself proud
But I cannot seem to stay focused

Constant music is in my head
Drowning out the times I have cried, winced and bled
I often feel like I am so far ahead
But I catch myself trailing behind

Confidence may not be the key
Perhaps it's a mindset of reality
A balance of optimism and rationality
Because I don't know what the hell I am doing

Staticity wasn't in my will
But I would rather be walking in circles than standing still
The world is my prey and I'm here to kill
I just need to find out how

You asked me how many poems I have written about you
How many times I have exposed the heartache
How many times I spilled my love or my resentment for you on paper
My brow arched and I giggled
You never could tell if that was good or bad
and I said to you
 "Not more times than I have told you myself
but you never listened to me
so you would not know if they were about you
anyways"

So if you are reading this,
just know that this is for you.

Never say

THE END

Because you will always be
A work in progress

Special thanks to a good friend, Caleb Sachs for editing the tough, showing compassion for the tougher and supporting me for the toughest.

68997788R00063

Made in the USA
San Bernardino, CA
09 February 2018